Penny Bonadonna Donehoo is a retired occupational therapist. She immigrated, with her family, from a small village in Sicily to the United States when she was six months old. Currently, she lives in Mount Prospect, Illinois, with her husband. Luckily, their four children and eight grandchildren live close by, so she can spend her time babysitting and telling them stories.

This book is dedicated to the memory of my parents, Placido and Grace Bonadonna; and to my family – Paris, Rachel, Matthew, Meg, Kathryn, Natalie, Charlotte, Issac, Clare, Bethany, Morgan, Felix, and Murphy. I wrote these stories for you.

Penny Bonadonna Donehoo

A New Home and Other Stories

Austin Macauley Publishers

LONDON • CAMBRIDGE • NEW YORK • SHARJAH

A CIP catalogue record for this title is available from the British Library.

ISBN 9781035801060 (Paperback)
ISBN 9781035801077 (ePub e-book)

www.austinmacauley.com

First Published 2023
Austin Macauley Publishers Ltd®
1 Canada Square
Canary Wharf
London
E14 5AA

Thank you to Austin Macauley and their editors for helping me publish this book. My sister, Rosalie Musiala, deserves a thank you for agreeing to let me merge both of our personalities and experiences into the character 'Lina'. A special thank you to my husband, Paris, for listening to all my questions and providing so much support and love. A big hug and thank you go out to my son, Matthew Holihan, for his support and assistance with computers and social media. Thank you to the rest of my children, Rachel Georgakis; my stepdaughters, Meg Pfister and Kathryn Keenon. This book was written for my grandchildren, Natalie, Charlotte, Isaac, Clare, Bethany, Morgan, Felix, and Murphy. This book is a part of their history too. Finally, thank you to Papa and Mama for bringing me to America. I miss you every day.

Table of Contents

Foreword

The stories in this book are basically true. They are based on events that happened to me and my family. However, I owe my sister, Rosalie, an apology because the character 'Lina' is a combination of myself and my sister. Some of the names have been changed and stories combined. My family immigrated to the United States of America from Ventimiglia, Sicily, when I was six months old and my sister was seven years old. Some of these events happened to me and some to her, and some to others in our family. I have written this book for my grandchildren. They should know a little about their heritage and ancestors. This is also a thank you to my parents, Placido and Grazia Bonadonna, for having the courage and determination to bring us to a new country.

A New Home

Grazia slammed the door shut with tears gathering in the corners of her eyes.

This is it, she thought, *the end of everything I know.* She looked down the street toward the yellowish-brown mountains rising up at the end of the village street. Taking a deep breath, Grazia pulled her daughter Lina's hand toward the truck waiting in front of their house. No, not their house anymore. She had sold it to the Santorini family. Tilting her chin up and holding back the tears, Grazia helped Lina onto the seat of the truck.

"Are we going to have a bigger house in America?" Lina asked.

"Of course, my little one, someday," Grazia said, patting Lina's thigh as she slid into the seat next to her. "One thing at a time, though. We have to get to the ship first."

Turning toward the driver, Grazia said, "Let's get going." It was better to not drag out the pain of leaving. *I want to go and yet, it still hurts,* she thought.

The truck began rumbling down the cobblestone street and out of their small Sicilian village. Ventimiglia had been Grazia and Lina's home for all their lives. The farthest the two of them had ever gone was Parlemo, the nearby city only twenty miles away. Now, they were going on a big ship across the Atlantic Ocean.

Grazia smiled bravely at her seven-year-old daughter.

I can't let her see how frightened I am. If she starts to cry, I won't be able to hold back, Grazia thought as she took a deep breath, braced her arm against the truck's dashboard and began to look forward.

The truck's bouncing on the road made Lina giggle. She hadn't ridden in vehicles very much and this was fun. Grazia took a quick glance behind her to the truck bed, checking on the big brown trunk that contained all their belongings. "The back of the truck is closed tight, right?" she nervously asked the driver.

"Yes," responded the driver, Filippo. "I locked the back and strapped down the trunk. Don't worry, *Signora* (ma'am). I have driven many people to the steamship dock in Palermo. I haven't lost a single thing, yet."

"Mama, I smell olives," Lina said.

Filippo said, "Ah, little one, that's because my truck usually carries the farmers' olives to the markets and olive oil factories."

"My papa grows almonds. He's a farmer too."

Grazia corrected her daughter. "Not anymore. Your papa is working in America now." Looking out the window at the countryside, Grazia saw a lonely stone hut in the middle of an abandoned field. "That's what's happened all over Italy," Grazia thought aloud. "The war has made it harder for people to make a living. Farmers can't make enough money anymore and they leave their farms for work elsewhere."

"That's true." Filippo agreed. "I spend as much time driving people into Parlemo to the ships and trains as I do driving olives and almonds to their destination. Having a truck has been a blessing. It has made it possible for my family to continue living in Sicily."

"Mama, wasn't the war a long time ago?" Lina was confused. She knew there had been a war but it was before she was born.

"Oh, Lina. It ended nine years ago but Italy has had a hard time rebuilding. It has been very hard to make a decent living. Things will be better for us in America. Your papa is waiting for us there. Oh, look, there's Palermo." Grazia pointed to the tall buildings in the distance rising out of the ground ahead of them. *Forward,* she thought. *I have to keep looking forward.*

Lina's brown eyes became as big as saucers as she stared at all the folks leaning against the rail of the ship. "Mama, where did all these people come from? Are they all going to America?" She had never seen so many bodies in one place.

"Yes, little one. They are all on this ship, The Vulccania, because it's sailing to America. Some are going to find a better life, some to visit someone, some are going home. Lots of different reasons. But you need to stay next to me." Grazia put her arm around Lina's shoulder and pulled her in closer. "I don't want you to get lost. It's a big ship."

Lina pushed onto her tiptoes to see over the railing. One of her long brown braids plopped over the railing edge as she looked toward the front of the ship. The dark blue side of the ship seemed to stretch a thousand miles. She couldn't see the end of it. "Mama, this ship looks longer than our street in Ventimiglia!"

Trying not to be overwhelmed herself, Grazia peered over the railing in the direction Lina was looking. "It's supposed to be four blocks long. I read that in the brochure Papa left us with the tickets." Clutching her satchel close, which was filled with the clothes they would wear during the voyage, Grazia pulled Lina away from the railing. "Let's go find our cabin."

"What's a cabin, Mama?" Lina asked as she held tightly onto her mother's hand, looking from side to side at all the wondrous sights around her.

"It's the room we are going to sleep in. Every family has their own cabin. It's like having your own little house in this big town of a ship." Grazia found the stairwell and slowly began going down the steps while holding Lina's hand.

Forward, I have to keep looking forward, she thought as her heart was looking backward at the only home she had ever known. She was determined not to let Lina sense her own fear.

Lina had never seen so many stairs. Looking over the handrail she saw the stairs going on and on as if into the center of the earth. "Mama, do we have to walk down all of them?"

The amazement in Lina's voice was mixed with a touch of unease.

"No. Just to level six."

Climbing slowly down the stairs Grazia and Lina soon found themselves on the level numbered six. Looking down the hallway there were so many doors with numbers on them.

"Do all these doors have rooms for sleeping?" asked Lina.

"Yes, yes," Grazia wearily replied. She was looking forward to laying down and closing her eyes for a few minutes.

They continued walking down the seemingly endless hallway. "Ah, here it is. 6645." Grazia set down her satchel and dug into her purse for the key she had been given at the registration desk. She slid it into the keyhole and slowly opened the door. Lina bounded into the room.

"Oh! It's a very small home, Mama!" Lina stood in the middle of the room with her arms outstretched. Her fingertips were nowhere near the walls but Grazia's would be close in the same position.

Grazia looked at the bed with a blue bedspread on it, sticking out from the wall right in front of her. It was big enough for her, but looked a little small for the two of them together. Above it was another smaller bed, with the same bedspread, also attached to the wall.

Throwing herself onto the lower bunk, Lina exclaimed, "Look, Mama! The wall has beds growing from it!"

Placing her satchel in the corner, Grazia sat down gently on the corner of the bed. "Lina be careful. This bed belongs to the ship."

"A ladder!" Lina bounced to the end of the bed where the ladder to the upper bunk was attached. "Can I climb it? Please! Mama, Please!" Lina pleaded.

Grazia sighed. "Okay. Be careful. That will be where you will sleep." Grazia could not imagine herself sleeping on that 'floating' bed and Lina seemed delighted with the prospect.

Lina quickly climbed up the ladder and threw herself onto the upper bunk bed.

"It's like sleeping in the sky," she exclaimed. "I can see everything from up here."

Stretching out on the bottom bunk, Grazia scanned the narrow cabin and gazed at the bottom of the bed above her. "There's not much to see."

"Oooh. There's another door!" Lina noticed an oval frame opening with a door in it. Scurrying down the ladder, she asked, "What's in here, Mama?"

"I don't know. Try the door knob." Grazia pointed to a metal half circle on the left side of the door.

Carefully, Lina wrapped her fingers around the metal semicircle and pulled. Nothing happened. The door remained closed.

"Push it," instructed Grazia. Lina held the metal and pushed. Nothing happened. "Try turning it. Careful, though." Grazia didn't want to start this voyage with Lina breaking something. Gently, Lina rotated her wrist while still holding the metal. The door 'click-clicked' as it opened.

"Oh, Mama, look!" Lina stepped into the bathroom. "Is this the toilet?" Lina's voice was full of wonder.

"Ah! We have our own bathroom!" Grazia said with delight. "I thought we might have to share one with other passengers." Grazia got up from her bed, being careful to not bump her head on the top bunk. "Let me show you how it works. I've seen bathrooms like this in Palermo." Grazia stepped into the tiny bathroom, forcing Lina to step into the shower stall because of the lack of floor space. Grazia put her hand on the toilet handle, "After you use the toilet, you push this handle down." Grazia explained as she flushed the toilet.

"There's water coming in there!" Lina was so surprised. It was nothing like the outhouse they had behind their house in Ventimiglia.

Grazia then turned the handle on the small sink. "This is how you wash your hands."

Lina's mouth fell open as she watched her mother demonstrate washing her hands under the running water of the

17

faucet. "We don't have to fetch water from a pump and use a pitcher?" Lina's voice got louder and louder with her excitement. "What's this I am standing in, then?" Lina spun around in the shower. "Look, here's some more handles, like those where you washed your hands." Lina turned the knobs right in front of her. *Splutter, whirr, splush,* went the water coming out of the showerhead above Lina.

"Aughh!" gasped Grazia as she turned the handle off and pulled a wet Lina out of the shower. "You're all wet!" Grazia grabbed one of the towels from the rack within the bathroom and began patting Lina dry. "That must be the shower I have heard people talking about. You stand in there with the water running and wash yourself."

"They don't have a metal tub, like we use at home? How do we heat the water?" Lina was very confused.

"The handles are marked for cold and hot water. It comes out automatically when you turn the handle. That's how you got wet." Grazia picked up her satchel and pulled out Lina's pink striped dress and dry underclothes. "Put these on. It will be time for dinner soon. Let's get a little rest first. We will try out the shower tomorrow when we wash up. Leave it alone, now, Lina."

With her dry clothes on, Lina climbed up the ladder and carefully lay down so she wouldn't wrinkle her dress too much. "Mama, will we have a bathroom like this in America? Will we have our own water pouring inside our house? Mama?"

"Yes, Lina. From what I understand, most homes have sinks, toilets and showers with running water inside. Now, close your eyes. I need to rest." Grazia had already laid back on the bed and was trying to relax. The day had been almost more than she could handle.

Lina closed her eyes and thought, *already, America is full of surprises.*

The dining room of the ship is larger than our church in Ventimiglia! Thought Lina as she sat down at a table covered with a white cotton tablecloth. The room was bustling with people being seated and waiters bringing in platters of food. Grazia's eyes widened as she took in the scene around her. She had never been to a restaurant and wasn't sure of what she should do.

"*Ciao, mi chiamo* Elena (hello, my name is Elena)." A friendly voice interrupted Grazia's worried thoughts. Grazia turned toward the speaker and saw a middle-aged woman with grey streaks in her shoulder length black hair.

"*Ciao.* My name is Grazia Amatiza. This is my daughter, Lina," she responded.

Elena sat down at their table and proceeded to get acquainted. "I am returning to New York after visiting my parents in Cefalu. I hadn't seen them in over ten years. How about you? Is this your first trip across the ocean?"

"We're going to meet my papa in America!" Lina piped in before Grazia got an opportunity to gather her thoughts. "He's going to have a house for us with water coming right into the sink!"

Elena laughed. "Yes, I am sure your papa will. Is your papa in New York?"

Grazia gently placed her hand over Lina's, signaling she needed to be quiet.

"My husband, Paolo, is in Chicago. His brother has been living there for a number of years and is an American citizen.

19

We've waited a long time for the immigration papers to clear so we can go to America too. But when the papers came through there was a problem with how they wrote Lina's name and we had to wait for it to get straightened out." Grazia's voice became more anxious as she rambled on with each sentence. "Paolo left first. Silvestro, Paolo's brother, also helped my husband find a job in Chicago and now we are going there to live. First, we will see my uncle in New York. I haven't seen him since I was a child. I don't know if he will recognize me. Then we will take a train to Chicago to be with Paolo." She was talking faster and faster. Grazia hadn't realized how truly worried she was. There had been so much to do to get ready to travel that she hadn't allowed herself time to fret.

Elena put her arm around Grazia's shoulders and gently whispered. "Don't worry. Have faith. Things will get better. I have been where you are. It will work out." Looking at Lina, "How about we get something to eat? There's the buffet table." Elena pointed across the room to a long table full of steaming dishes.

"Can we just go get the food?" asked Grazia.

"Yes," answered Elena "Just follow me."

Grazia took Lina's hand in hers and walked closely behind Elena's confident stride. Elena picked up a white dinner plate from a stack in a large brown plastic container. The knives, forks and spoons were each standing up in what looked like tall metal cups without handles. Elena took one from each. Grazia picked up a plate from the very same stack and placed another plate in Lina's hand.

"Be careful, Lina. Don't drop it." Grazia told her daughter. "Oh, good! They have pasta." Grazia put some on each of their plates.

"There's lots of other things too, Mama. Look, what's that yellow stick?" Lina asked.

"That's a banana." Elena answered before Grazia could. "They're delicious. Try it." Elena put one on Lina's plate and another on her own. "Do you want one?" Elena asked Grazia.

"No, thank you. I don't think I should try different foods today. My stomach isn't feeling that good." Grazia put a piece of Italian bread on her plate. "The bread might help."

"It could be the movement of the ship." Elena said as she led the way back to their table. "Sometimes, it feels like you're going up and down and sometimes you don't feel anything at all."

Lina sat in her chair and picked up the banana. "How do you eat it? Should I just bite it?" she asked Elena as she put the side of the banana up to her mouth.

"No, no, no!" exclaimed Elena as she took the banana out of Lina's hand. Elena peeled the banana halfway down. "Like this." She instructed. Handing the banana back to Lina, "You bite the inside and eat that part. The peel you throw away."

Lina held the banana in her hand. She was excited to try something new. Taking a big bite, Lina's nose filled with the aroma of the banana. It was like nothing she had ever smelled before. Suddenly, the floor of the dining room felt like it dropped away from Lina's chair. "Mama!" Lina cried out with her mouth full of the banana. The typical dining room chatter became overpowered with the loud gasps of the fellow passengers.

"Oh, Mother of God." Grazia prayed as she hugged Lina close to her.

Elena pointed to one of the small round windows on one side of the dining room. "Look, it's just the waves on the ocean." The horizon line outside the window was no longer level. "That happens every now and then. We will be fine."

Lina's stomach felt like it was tilting like the view from the dining room window. She picked up her napkin and spit the banana into it like her mother had shown her to do, if she didn't like something.

"Bananas smell bad," Lina said as she placed the scrunched-up napkin onto the table. "Maybe, I won't like everything in America!"

The next morning Grazia's fingers lightly brushed the wall as she stretched her arms overhead. She had been so tired when she went to bed the night before that she immediately fell asleep. Her eyes fluttered open and fixed on the brown metal of the bunk over her head. Lina's bed. It was quiet in the cabin. *Lina must still be asleep,* Grazia thought. As Grazia swung her legs from the bed onto the floor she remembered waking up in the middle of the night as the boat rocked side to side. She had been so worn out from all the changes that she rolled over and fell back to sleep.

"Lina, let's go try that shower!" called Grazia as she stood up. No one answered her. Grazia stood on her tiptoes and peered into the top bunk. The covers were all jumbled in the middle of the bunk. Grazia stepped up onto the lower bunk to give her short five-foot frame some extra inches. "Lina?" She cautiously poked the pile of bedding. Nothing. No child. "How can this be? Where is she?" Grazia began to worry. *Oh,* she thought, *she probably snuck down the ladder and is playing with the shower in the bathroom. She doesn't hear me.*

Grazia took the two steps to the bathroom. "Lina, what are you doing in there?" The bathroom was empty and quiet. Grazia had expected to hear the water from the shower head splashing against the tiled walls and floor. Carefully pulling back the shower curtain, "Lina?" Grazia's worried voice called out. "Lina! Where are you?" Grazia was beginning to get scared. "Where could she be? This cabin is so small that I can't miss seeing her in it!" Grazia nervously opened the cabin door.

If Lina decided to walk around the ship by herself, I will never find her. It's so big! She wouldn't go walking around by herself. Grazia's mind raced as she looked up and down the narrow hallway. There was no one in the hallway.

"Where would Lina go?" Grazia said to herself as she walked back into the cabin. She climbed up the ladder to the upper bunk, just to make sure she hadn't missed Lina's thin seven-year-old body. Pulling the covers off the bed, Grazia was beginning to panic. Quickly climbing back down the ladder, she plopped herself down onto her bed, *Think, think! What can I do to find her? Who can I get to help me? Oh, Mother of God!* Grazia made the sign of the cross on her body as she did in church.

Screech, came a sound from under Grazia's bed.

"Oh, no! Lina's missing and I have mice in here too!" Taking a deep breath, Grazia gathered her courage and knelt down on the floor and peeked under the bed. "Oh, thank God!" Grazia gushed. There was Lina! She was just beginning to stir as she was waking up. Grazia reached in and pulled Lina out onto her lap. Cradling her like she did when Lina was a little baby, "Lina, what were you doing under the bed. I've been so frightened! I've been looking everywhere for you."

Lina cuddled into her Mother's arms. She looked up at Grazia, "Good morning, Mama."

"Did you get out of bed last night and crawl under my bed?"

"No, Mama. I stayed in bed like you told me to. I did scrunch down to the bottom where that bar stops." Lina pointed to an eighteen-inch gap from the foot of the upper bunk to the protective bar that ran alongside the bed. "That bar felt cold on my leg and I kept bumping it."

"You've always tossed and turned a lot in your sleep but you've been able to sleep through anything. Apparently, you slept through the rocking of the ship knocking you to the floor. You must have rolled under my bed in your sleep," Grazia concluded.

"That's funny. I slept under your bed!" Lina laughed.

"It wasn't funny. I was so scared. I thought you left the cabin and I wouldn't be able to find you." Grazia was practically crying with fear and joy.

"Silly, Mama! I wouldn't leave you. We're going to America together!" Lina planted a kiss on her Mama's cheek.

A week later, Lina held her hand over her eyebrows as she scanned the people crowding the ship's rails. "I see lots of buildings, Mama. They're so tall! Like giant blocks across the edge of the ocean."

"That's New York City. That's where my Uncle Andrea lives. He's supposed to meet us when we're done at Ellis Island." Grazia's shoulders sank a little more thinking about the long day they had ahead of them.

"What's Ellis Island, Mama?" Lina leaned forward to see her mother's face. "It's where they check our papers and make sure we are healthy enough to enter America. If you're sick there's a hospital there where you stay until you get better or sometimes, they send people back home."

"Is everyone on the ship going to Ellis Island, Mama?" Lina asked.

"No. The first and second-class passengers usually get right off the ship. We're third class so we have to go to Ellis Island to make sure we're healthy enough. You just stay right by my side. This is going to take a while." Grazia tried to sound upbeat but she was dreading the next few hours.

"So, third class people aren't as healthy?" Lina sounded confused.

"No honey, that's not it. It's just that first- and second-class passengers paid more for their tickets." Grazia tried to explain.

"Then they're wealthy and healthy. Wealthy and healthy." Lina began to sing.

"Lina! Stop that. Please try and be quiet." Grazia looked around her nervously.

Later Lina was no longer playful. She held her Mother's hand tightly. She was glad she was done going through all those lines and stations at Ellis Island. Lina had waited patiently with her mother, sometimes sitting on wooden benches and sometimes standing in long lines waiting for their names to be called. When the man with the long white jacket that Mama had said was a doctor lifted her dress and touched her chest with that cold metal circle, Lina felt like crying. But she didn't. Mama said they were just making sure she was healthy. *It was scary,* Lina thought. *I didn't understand what they were saying to me and they were touching me like I was their pillow or something.*

"Look, Lina," Grazia dropped Lina's hand and pointed to an old man in a brown tweed cap standing next to a stack of large wooden boxes. "I think that's Uncle Andrea." Grazia began waving her arm and yelling, "*Zio! Zio!* (Uncle, Uncle) I'm Grazia!" She reached down for Lina's hand again and practically dragged her. She ran to the older man with the brown cap.

"Grazia? Is it you?" The man looked into Grazia's face and placed his hands on either side of her cheeks. "It is you! I can see my sister, Providenza, in your face!" He gently kissed both sides of Grazia's face.

"Oh, *Zio*! I am so happy to finally be here." Grazia threw her arms around her Uncle's neck and hugged him tight.

"This must be Lina." Zio Andrea bent down and lightly kissed Lina's cheek.

"You speak Italian!" Lina screeched with delight. "I thought I wouldn't understand you, just like all those people at Ellis Island."

"Oh, Lina. I came from Italy many, many years ago. I speak English and Italian, just like you will." Zio Andrea gently tapped the top of Lina's head. "Well, let's get you home. Your Zia Pepina has her famous lasagna waiting for you. Later, I'll take you to my store and get some better coats. You'll never make it through a Chicago winter with those thin jackets."

After their delicious meal, they all piled into Zio Andrea's car to go to his store. Lina's brown eyes widened as they never had before. There were so many things to look at. Turning her head from one side to the other she felt she couldn't possibly see all the wonderful things around her. The streets were lined with bright lights overhead. It made the evening seem like daytime. There were so many cars on the road in front of her and they all had bright red lights on the back of them. The stores along the street had their signs in lights too. It reminded Lina of all the lights in the piazza when there was a festival in Ventimiglia.

"Zio, does your store have lights on the sign too?" Lina asked her Great Uncle Andrea.

"Of course, it does." Zio Andrea explained as he pulled in front of a building that had 'Andrea's Department Store' in blue lights across the front.

"You don't need to do this, Zio." Grazia protested as she got out of the front seat of the car. "We have coats. We will be fine."

Zio Andrea grabbed Grazia's hand with one hand and opened the back door of the car for Lina with the other. "Now, Grazia. Stop it. I am giving you coats from my store. You will need something warmer. It gets very cold in Chicago. And, it's the least I can do for my sister's daughter. I haven't seen her since I left Ventimiglia when I was fourteen, but she has written to me every week. I can still feel her love for me. Let me do this." Zio Andrea's eyes were beginning to tear up.

"Thank you, Zio. This is very kind of you." Grazia went up on her tiptoes and gave her uncle a kiss on his weathered cheek.

They walked into the store and Zio Andrea locked the door behind them.

"Ooooh," squealed Lina, as she twirled around in the center aisle looking at the dressed mannequins. "They're all so pretty!"

"The children's coats are back here," instructed Zio Andrea as he led them to the rear of the store. Lina reached out a cautious finger and touched the sleeve of a dark blue wool coat on the rack in front of her. Grazia gave Lina the stern look that all children understand to mean 'don't touch'. Zio Andrea pulled the blue coat off the rack. It had a red trim down the front and a matching blue wool hat with the same red trim on the edge.

"What's this?" asked Lina, as she pointed to the white fur muff hanging by a silver nylon cord from the coat hanger.

"That's a muff," Zio replied. "You put your hands in it to keep them warm in the cold air." He stuck his large hand into the child sized muff and wiggled his fingers that stuck out the other end. Lina giggled. She looked up at her Mother and said, "Can I try it on?"

Grazia nodded and Lina quickly slipped her arms into the coat as her Great Uncle held the coat out for her. The princess line shape of the coat fell gently over Lina's slim form. "Oh, Mama, it's so pretty!"

Grazia checked the length and shoulders. "It looks like she'll have a little room for growing into it too. Does it feel warm?" she asked her daughter.

"It's wonderful!" said Lina as she spun around causing the bottom of the coat to flare out.

"Lina stop that. You need to be careful with the things in Zio's store," scolded Grazia.

"It's okay." Laughed Zio Andrea. "Try on the hat and the muff." He handed them to Lina. "Do you like the color, Lina?"

"I love it!" Lina gushed as she hugged the coat.

Zio Andrea pulled the tags off and slipped them into his pocket. "You can wear the coat home. It's cold outside. This coat is better for the fall and spring," he said as he handed Grazia Lina's grey corduroy jacket. "Now for your coat, Grazia."

They walked back toward the other side of the store to the women's department. Grazia began looking through a rack of wool coats. She pulled a black one off the rack and held it up to herself. "This looks about the right size," she said as she looked up at her Uncle. "Oh, no!"

Uncle Andrea was standing a few feet in front of her holding a dark brown fur coat. "How about this?" he said with a twinkle in his eye.

"Mama, that looks like the ladies in your magazines!" Lina ran over and gently ran her hand down the long fur on the front of the coat. "Oh, it's so soft. Mama, feel it."

"Zio, that's too much." Grazia protested as Zio Andrea put the black coat back on the rack and held the fur coat out for Grazia to slip on.

"Mama, you look like a movie star!" Lina skipped around her mother with excitement. The collarless fur coat with the wide sleeves looked like it had been made for Grazia.

Grazia ran her hand down the sleeve and looked up at her Uncle. "No, Zio. It's too much."

Zio Andrea, pulled the tags off the fur coat. "Too late. It's yours," he said with a mischievous grin. He took Grazia's and Lina's thin coats from Italy and placed them in a bag. "Okay, let's go home in warm coats."

"Zio, let me pay for them. I do have some money from the farm. I sold it after Paolo left for America. I have that money with me." Grazia pleaded with her Uncle.

"No. And that's final. Now, let's go back home and have some coffee and cannoli. Then, Lina, you'll need to go to bed. Your train to Chicago is early in the morning."

"A new coat, cannoli, a train ride, and I see Papa again!" Lina hugged her Uncle. "America is fun!"

Lina had her nose pressed against the train window with her fingertips against the glass. "Look, Mama. I can see tall buildings."

"Yes, Lina. Maybe, you shouldn't keep your head so close to the window."

"Will Papa be there when we get off the train?" Lina couldn't wait to see her father and show him her new coat. She had so many things to tell him about.

"He's supposed to meet us at the train station. He promised. Zio Silvestro and Zia Mary will be with him. We will be living upstairs from them." Grazia's voice was shaky. The movement of the train had made her nervous and now that they were getting closer to their final destination, she was even more anxious. Her new life was really going to start.

"Mama?"

"What, little one?" Grazia leaned her head down.

"I love you," she said and kissed her Mother's nose.

"I love you, too." Grazia sighed. "We'll be together. It's going to be alright."

"Does Zio Silvestro have a store like Zio Andrea?"

"No, sweetheart. Zio Andrea was very lucky and he worked hard. Not everyone in America lives like Zio Andrea does." Grazia worried her daughter would have unrealistic expectations now.

"It feels like we're stopping," Lina jumped down from the weathered brown leather seat.

30

The train lurched back as it stopped throwing Lina off balance. Grazia grabbed her by the shoulders. "You have to stay right next to me and hold my hand. There will be a lot of people." She gathered her things and took Lina by the hand. Standing on the top step leading down from the train, Grazia could see people crowded along the train platform. Carefully, Grazia stepped down and helped her daughter off the step.

"Mama, your coat is so soft," Lina ran her fingers down the full sleeves of her mother's coat.

Grazia stood still and looked down the platform. "There he is! Look, Lina. There's Papa." She pointed at Paolo who was craning his neck side to side looking over the sea of faces for his family. Grazia and Lina began to walk down the platform as quickly as they could.

"Thank goodness we have these warm coats, Mama," Lina said as the cold Chicago wind blew across their faces. "Zio Andrea was right. It is cold in Chicago!"

"Paolo, Paolo!" Grazia called waving her arm as she walked closer and closer.

"Grazia!" Lina heard her father's voice. "Mama! It's Papa!" Lina ran to her father. She threw her arms around his legs. Paolo reached down and patted his daughter's back. Grazia threw her arms around her husband's neck and buried her face into his shoulder, "Oh, Paolo! I've missed you so much!"

Paolo gently laid his hand on Grazia's shoulder and fingered the fur coat. He looked into her deep brown eyes which were brimming with tears. "What have you done with the money from the farm? Look at these coats! What have you done, Grazia?"

Grazia burst out laughing. "Oh, Paolo. Don't I deserve a kiss first? I didn't buy these. Don't worry." She gave her husband a kiss and said, "They're from my Uncle Andrea in New York. The money from the farm is safe."

Paolo picked up his wife and twirled her around. "Thank goodness. I was worried when I saw you! I thought you squandered our money on clothes."

Lina's Aunt Mary reached over and gently touched Grazia's new coat. She turned toward her husband, Silvestro, "I've been in America my whole life and I don't have a fur coat."

Silvestro ignored his wife and looked at Paolo. "Let's get their luggage and get you all home."

At last the reunited Amatiza family arrived at the three-story brick building on the north side of Chicago. "Oh, Papa," Lina gushed, "it's so big!"

Paolo laughed, "It's not all our home, little one. Three families live here. Your Uncle Silvestro and Aunt Mary live on the first floor. They own the whole building. Another family rents the second floor. We live all the way up on top in the attic on the third floor. Uncle Silvestro fixed it up for us." Paolo pointed to the top floor close to the slanting roof. They climbed the open staircase in the back of the building. Paolo opened the door with a gold colored key. "You have to always lock the door here. It's not like Ventimiglia where everyone keeps their doors open."

"It's too cold here to keep your doors open," said Grazia as she wrapped her arms around her new coat.

Lina followed her Mama into the three-room apartment. "Papa, watch out, your head will hit the ceiling." Lina pointed to the slanted ceiling barely clearing her father's head.

"Don't worry. I have walked all around here and I haven't hit my head yet. But I can't jump up and down." Paolo lightly slid his hand over his head. "Here's the bedroom." Paolo pointed to the room off the kitchen/living room area. There was a double bed and inside the large closet there was a twin bed mattress on the floor.

"That's your bed, Lina," Paolo said. "There's something for you on it."

Lina squealed with delight. There was a red rubber ball sitting on the pillow.

Lina grabbed the ball and began jumping on the mattress. "Look, I can almost touch the roof."

"Stop that!" scolded Grazia. "Let's get your coat off and unpack."

When the new coats had been hung in the closet, Lina ran into the bathroom and began running the water in the sink.

"This is mine," she said as she ran her fingers under the faucet. "Mama, look! We do have a shower, toilet, and sink like Zio Andrea and the boat had!" Lina walked back into the bedroom and looked out the window. Then she turned around and saw her blue wool coat and her Mama's fur coat hanging in the little closet. "My new home is up high in the sky where lots of good things are possible."

Where's the Angel?

Chicago, 1956

"Where's the angel, Mama?" Lina's excited voice matched the bouncing of her feet clad in her shiny dress shoes.

"It's not time yet." Lina's mother, Grazia, replied wearily. They had just descended from the green and white city bus and walked a few feet to the Italian Festival.

Lina pulled on her mother's arm, "You said we would see the angels."

"They aren't real angels. I've already explained it. It's re-enactment, like a live TV show. The angels are little girls, about eight or nine years old, about your age, they are dressed up in angel costumes. Back home in Ventimiglia, the angels are hooked up to wires above the piazza and it looks like they are really flying high above our heads. I don't know if they do it the same here in America." Grazia had explained all this to Lina on the bus ride. Lina focused on the idea of seeing angels and totally ignored the connection to festivals in the town in Sicily where she was born.

"Lina, what does that sign say? Do we have to pay to get in?" asked Lina's father. Lina could speak and read English much better than her parents. It hadn't taken her long to learn the language. She frequently had to translate for her parents.

"No, Papa. The festival is free. The sign just says this is the entrance and the bathrooms are behind that trailer." Lina responded.

Paolo helped guide Grazia and Lina through the bright yellow sawhorses which were placed across the beginning of the street.

"Will the angels be walking around, Papa?" asked Lina, scanning the crowd.

"It's an Italian festival. They will probably do it like they do in Italy. Like your Mama explained on the bus. Just listen, it's like being back home." Accordion music was playing in the distance and they could hear some people talking in the Sicilian dialect of her village.

"Papa, you're wrong," Lina said with delight. She loved correcting her parents. "I hear some English, too."

"Of course." Paolo responded. "You don't think Americans would miss a chance for some good Italian food?" Turning toward Grazia, "Do you think we can get a decent cannolo? I haven't had one since you made them for my brother's birthday. Thank goodness you brought the cannoli forms with you from Italy. I haven't seen those in the stores here."

"I packed as much as I could in that big brown trunk. Now let's start looking at what there is to eat." Grazia took Lina's hand in hers. "Don't let go. Stay with me. It's not like in the Ventimiglia, where you can walk around by yourself."

Holding her mother's hand, Lina looked down the street. Brightly colored triangular flags crisscrossed overhead. They flapped gently in the breeze. No angels on them. There were colorful wooden stalls with food vendors scattered on both sides of the street. People were lined up in front of them. The street, which usually would have vehicles traveling along it, was filled with small groups of people casually dressed, chatting and eating. Lina could smell the aromas of some of her favorite Italian foods such as Italian beef, Italian sausage, and meatball sandwiches. But she didn't see any angels. There was a stall with toys that lit up when you pushed a plunger on the underside. That was pretty interesting but Lina kept looking down the street, behind the crowds. She was looking for angels and was determined to find one.

"Ah, there they are." Paolo pointed to a stall across the road. It had biscotti and cannoli piled onto silver trays. "Let's get in line." Paolo didn't even wait for a response from his family as he strode across the street to get into the long line in front of the pastry vendor.

Grazia followed with Lina in tow. "Now, Lina," she said as she bent down to Lina's face. "You can only pick one thing to eat at the festival. We don't have a lot of money. So, if you want some cannoli, no gelato later. We had lunch at home and will eat dinner when we get back home. You can pick one treat."

"What would the angel eat, Mama?" Lina asked. "Because, that's what I want."

"Cannoli, then. Paolo, get three cannoli. Angels love cannoli."

Suddenly, Lina heard someone yelling. "No! Stop it!" She looked up and across from her she saw a group of older boys. They were behind two of the food stands. The boys looked about the age of the boys that walked into the high school at the end of her block. The tallest boy was holding the back of a much smaller boy's shirt. He was tugging on it so hard that the smaller boy's voice came out in choked sobs. The bully's other arm was pushing the smaller boy to the ground. "Please! Stop!" The smaller boy pleaded as his arms swung wildly at his sides.

"Check his pockets." The tall boy demanded of his partners in crime.

"Mama, look." Lina pointed to the brawling boys between the food stands. Grazia didn't understand what the boys were saying, but she clearly understood what was happening. Dropping Lina's hand, Grazia quickly dodged through the crowd who seemed unaware of the disturbance. Grazia planted her feet firmly in front of the tallest boy.

"*Ma che cosa stai facendo!* (What are you doing!)" Grazia yelled in Italian as she took hold of the smaller boy's arm with her right hand and helped him stand.

"*Fermati! Sei una vergogna!* (Stop! You're a disgrace!)" Grazia waved her left arm at the hoodlums as if she were shooing flies from a dinner table. "*Vai! Vattini!* (Go! Get out of here!)" The tall boy was so startled by Grazia's anger that he let go of his victim.

The smaller boy stumbled, but Grazia held his arm and kept him from landing in the dirt again. He quickly hid behind Grazia's blue flowered dress.

With her heart pounding in her chest, Lina tugged on Paolo's sleeve and then pointed toward the scuffle. Her father had been so focused on purchasing his beloved cannoli that he hadn't noticed the nearby assault.

"What is your mother doing?" Paolo demanded.

Grazia waved her arms, stomped her foot, and shrieked at the boys again. "*Vai! Ti avevo detto di uscire di qui!* (Go! I told you to get out of here!)"

The offending boys began to back away. "You're crazy, lady," muttered the tallest boy. "Let's get out of here," he growled to his sidekicks as they melted into the crowd.

Grazia brushed off the smaller boy's t-shirt which had a picture of a hot dog on it, now with a smudge of dirt over the mustard. She helped the boy pick up the contents of his pockets that had been strewn on the ground. "Here," she said in her heavily accented English, as she placed the coins into the boy's hands.

"Thanks, lady." The boy's voice trembled.

"Mama? Papa?" Grazia asked as she gestured toward the oblivious crowd in the street.

"I'm okay. Thank you. I'll be alright. Thank you again, lady." The boy seemed embarrassed and clearly wanted to leave. He stepped away from Grazia, smiled at her as he disappeared into the crowd.

"Grazia!" called Paolo. "What are you doing?"

Papa sounds angry, thought Lina.

"That boy needed help," said Grazia as she approached Lina and Paolo who were still standing in the pastry stand line. "Those brats were picking on him and stealing his money."

"You didn't need to get in the middle of that. There were three of them. They could have hurt you!" Paolo scolded.

"Well, no one else was doing anything to help. And I'm fine, aren't I?" retorted Grazia.

"You are always acting without thinking of what could happen. You need to be more careful," chided Paolo.

Lina worried her parents were going to have an argument in the middle of the street.

"Next." The tired voice behind the pastry stand counter rang out.

"Three," Paolo said in Italian as he held up three fingers.

Thank goodness for cannoli, thought Lina as they walked away munching on the sweet dessert. Papa obviously was upset about Mama helping that boy, but eating cannoli seemed to calm everybody down. Now, Lina could look for the angels again.

The crowd was getting thicker as they walked down the middle of the street. Up ahead Lina saw thick black wires crossing high over people's heads. *Maybe that's where the angels will fly,* thought Lina. Looking downward from the wires was a tall statue of Mary, Jesus' Mother. The statue was on a cart that had been decorated with flowers all around it. Lina tried to get closer to it. Maybe the angels were waiting under the cart. It would be fun to catch the angels there. But Grazia was holding her hand tightly.

"Lina, you need to stay next to us. You can get lost in the middle of all those people." Grazia pulled Lina over to the side of the street. She leaned against a telephone pole.

"I can't see, Mama," protested Lina. "There's too many people. Are the angels there yet? I want to see their pretty dresses and wings."

A man's loud voice came out over a speaker and spilled over the crowd. People's chattering voices started to fade away as the voice announced the beginning of the festival's presentation.

"It's starting, Lina. I'll pick you up." Paolo lifted Lina over his head and onto his shoulders.

"Thanks, Papa. I can see everything from up here." Lina scanned the crowd around her. No angels. She looked down, thinking maybe the angels were sneaking through the throng of people. There standing just a few feet away from her was the young boy Grazia had rescued. It had to be him. He was wearing the t-shirt with the picture of a hot dog on it and the smudge of dirt over the mustard.

"Lina, look there," called Grazia's voice as she pointed toward the overhead wires.

"Ohhhh, yes! There they are! There are the angels!" Lina squealed with delight. Two little girls were hooked to wires descending from the heavy tall poles from which the wires going across the street were connected to. One little girl was dressed in a pink flowing satin gown that reached the tips of her feet. It had long flowing sleeves and sparkling silvery wings which fanned out from the back of her gown. The other little girl had a matching gown in light blue. They were slowly being lifted up into the sky by the wires and harnesses strapped to their backs. "They're flying! The angels are flying!" Lina was entranced. "I wish I could be an angel like that!" shouted Lina to her Mother.

The boy with the hot dog shirt turned toward Lina's loud voice. He was looking up at Lina and then down to Grazia.

Lina, pointed to the soaring angels overhead and said to him, "Look! There are the angels!"

The boy gently pointed toward Grazia. "No. That's my angel."

The Amatiza Fruit and Vegetable Market

New York, 1909

"Apples, oranges, fresh tomatoes," Silvestro's father, Giuseppe, was singing on the busy street corner in the Little Italy section of New York City.

"We have lettuce and eggplant, too!" yelled Silvestro as he tried to help his father.

"Silvestro, go inside," Giuseppe gently nudged his son toward the fruit and vegetable market's front door. "Your mama will be walking you to school soon. Go get your things."

"But Papa, look, it's Franco." Silvestro pointed to a young man who was crossing the street and walking towards them. "I want to say, hi."

"Giuseppe, Silvestro, *ciao. Buon giorno.* (Hello. Good day). You both sound like peddlers from the old country. You're not going up and down the streets with your goods to sell. Here, in America, the people come to you."

"How are they going to know what I have to sell? The food is all inside. I picked it up early this morning." Giuseppe questioned his friend. This was the first week of the Amatiza family's fruit and vegetable market. Giuseppe was eager to make it a success.

Silvestro ran into the store and came back outside with a handful of grapes. "Look, Franco. I told Papa to get these green grapes. They're good!" Silvestro gushed as he popped a grape into his mouth.

Franco picked a grape and put it into his mouth. "Silvestro has the right idea. Bring some of your food out here on the sidewalk. Then people can see what you have to sell." Franco walked into the fruit and vegetable market. "These stands are pretty light. I'll help you move them outside."

"I'll help too, Papa. I'll hold the door." Silvestro pushed the front door open and held his seven-year-old body against it to keep it open. Franco and Giuseppe carried two stands outside.

"It's a good idea," Giuseppe said. "People will get hungry just walking past and maybe buy some. Also, it'll make room for some more things inside the shop."

Giuseppe was excited about his new store. Franco and Giuseppe had barely finished placing the apples on the outdoor stand when a customer stopped and asked how much the apples cost.

"You were right, Franco. This was a good idea." Giuseppe said as he put the money from the sale into his cash register. "In Ventimiglia we couldn't have the food outside for everyone to see. The donkeys going up and down the street would walk up and eat an apple right off the stand!" In the mountainous Sicilian village that Giuseppe had immigrated from, the farmers traveled to their mountain farms by donkey or horse which they kept in a stall next to their homes in the village.

"Papa, it was my idea, too. I brought the grapes outside."
Silvestro was as excited as his Papa.

"Yes, well, now it's time to go to school." Giuseppe
looked at his watch. "Go find your mama."

"Yes, Papa." Silvestro started toward the door, "Bye,
Franco."

"*Ciao.* (Good-bye) Silvestro." said Franco. "I have to get
going or I'll be late for work too." Franco walked away as
Giuseppe turned to help a customer who was looking at his
apples and pears.

A few weeks later, Silvestro was rolling a ball back and
forth to his little sister, Gina, while they were sitting on the
floor of their parents' market. Rosaria, Silvestro's mama, was
carrying pears to stack onto the outdoor stands.

"Open the door for me, Silvestro." Rosaria instructed. As
Silvestro opened the door for his mama, Gina threw the ball
and it rolled out the door right past Rosaria's feet.

"My ball!" Silvestro shouted as he saw his small red ball
roll away from the store's doorway. Just then Silvestro saw a
pair of shiny black shoes stop the ball from rolling onto the
street. The man with the black shoes picked up the ball and
walked toward Rosaria with the ball in his hand.

"*Grazie.* Thank you." Rosaria whispered. She wasn't very
comfortable speaking English and she didn't know if the man
spoke Italian, as most of the neighbors did.

"My ball!" Silvestro shouted again as he tried to reach for
the ball. The man held the red rubber ball in his large hand.

"Is this yours?" he calmly asked as he held Silvestro's ball
in one hand and then pointed to the store with his other hand
as he looked at Rosaria.

"*Si.* Yes." Rosaria said as she put down the pears she was holding. The man was tall and wore a gray hat. It looked like the one Giuseppe wore to church on Sundays.

"Nice store you have here," he said in Italian as he walked into the market while still holding the ball in his hand.

"Grazie," Rosaria said again. She gently took the ball out of the man's hand and gave it to her son. "Silvestro, take Gina to the kitchen." She gently pushed her son towards the back of the store.

The tall man took another look around the store. "Nice," he said as he walked out the front door.

"Papa, that man stopped my ball from going into the street." Silvestro said as he passed him while holding Gina's hand in one hand and his ball in the other.

"That was nice of him," Giuseppe said. Rosaria looked up at her husband. "Yes, but I don't know. There was something about him that made me feel uncomfortable. The way he pointed and looked at the store. It gave me a chill."

Silvestro looked at his mama's worried face. Just then his Papa rumpled the messy brown hair on Silvestro's head. "Don't worry about it! We got Silvestro's ball back. And he spoke Italian. He's one of us. Silvestro, get your school bag. It's time to go to school."

Over time Giuseppe's store had become popular in the neighborhood. It was doing so well that Giuseppe was able to hire his friend, Franco to work for him. Silvestro liked seeing Franco every day. One day while Franco was showing Silvestro how to juggle apples, the man with the gray hat came back. He walked in with another very tall man who was wearing a black suit jacket even though it was warm outside.

"*Ciao.* Can I help you?" Giuseppe walked up to the man in the gray hat. Silvestro snuck between two of the fruit stands to watch. He remembered how worried his mama was when the man in the gray hat had been in their store before.

"We have fresh peaches today." Giuseppe waved toward the peach stand beside him. The man in the gray hat picked up a peach. He began to toss it up and catch it in his hand. Silvestro wondered if the man also knew how to juggle.

"I am Pasquale and this is my friend, Stefano. Our job is to make sure all the shops in our neighborhood are safe. Giuseppe, that's your name?" The man in the gray hat had a firm loud voice. Silvestro didn't have any trouble hearing what he said while he tried to stay out of sight. Giuseppe stood straighter. "Yes, that's my name."

"I would hate to see something bad happen to your shop." Pasquale said as he continued to toss the peach in the air. The tall man leaned forward and held his hand in front of Silvestro's Papa's eyes. He rubbed his thumb over his fingers with the same hand.

"Think about it," Pasquale said. "I'll be back later this week. It's a nice place you have here." He caught the peach and bit it as he and Stefano walked out of the store.

He didn't pay for that, thought Silvestro as he stayed sitting between the two stands.

Giuseppe put his hand on Franco's arm. "We have a problem, Franco. Those men, Pasquale and Stefano, are bad. I left Sicily to get away from people like that."

"What do you mean? He stole a peach. That's not much." Franco said.

"No, Franco. He wants money. Money from us or he's going to hurt our business. Or us." Giuseppe spoke in a soft voice.

"Oh, no!" Franco plopped himself down onto an empty wooden crate that was standing on its side. "We're not making enough to be paying protection money. Maybe, we should call the police."

"We can't call the police. All he's done so far is take a peach. I don't want to pay him anything. I know how this works. No matter how much we give him, it won't be enough. It will always be more and more money he will want."

"Papa, I have some money in my piggy bank!" Silvestro crawled out from between the two stands. "You can have that."

"Oh, Silvestro! I didn't know you were here." Giuseppe bent down and hugged his son. "Don't you worry. Papa's going to take care of this." He picked up Silvestro and walked him back to the back of the store to the stairs which led up to their apartment. "Go on. Go see what your mama and Gina are doing." Giuseppe patted Silvestro's back so he'd go up the stairs. Silvestro went halfway up the stairs and stopped to listen.

Giuseppe thought Silvestro had gone into their apartment. He turned toward Franco. "I won't pay protection money to those crooks. I came to America for a better life for Rosaria and me. But now I have children and they were born here. They will have a better life." Giuseppe pointed upstairs. "In Sicily, you always had to pay some crook for something to get done or not done. I am not going to do that here. This is America." Giuseppe's voice was firm and strong.

Franco looked at Giuseppe. "Are you sure? I don't want to pay them either."

"Then, that's it. Done!" Giuseppe tossed Franco a peach, "Eat."

Silvestro slowly walked up the rest of the stairs. *That's good,* he thought. *I really want to buy a fire truck with the money in my piggy bank.*

A week later, Giuseppe was on his back porch throwing stones toward the grape arbor he had built at the back of his yard.

"Mama! Papa's throwing rocks again!" Silvestro ran into the kitchen telling on his papa.

"Giuseppe, what are you doing? I told you to stop that!" Rosaria came out onto the porch wiping her hands on the flowered apron.

"Those birds keep eating my grapes! I've worked too hard making that grape arbor and I am not growing grapes to feed those birds!"

Silvestro looked up into his father's face, "Papa the birds need to eat too," he said softly.

"Let them eat something else." Giuseppe grumbled.

Rosaria picked up the small bowl of rocks and handed it to her husband. "Put these back on the ground. Find another way to stop the birds. You'll hurt someone throwing rocks from here. Silvestro, you go help your papa. I have to knead the bread."

Giuseppe and Silvestro walked down the stairs and into the backyard. "Here, Silvestro, you put the rocks back. Your mama sent you with me to make sure I did what she said. I am going to check on my grapes." Silvestro watched his papa walk into the Amatiza Fruit and Vegetable Market garden.

Giuseppe not only liked selling fruit and vegetables, he liked growing them too. His garden had tomatoes, lettuce, green beans, onions and many different kinds of herbs but his favorite produce was his grapes. Giuseppe stood under his small grape arbor, reached up, plucked a ripe grape and put it in his mouth. "Maybe, if I had a fake hawk or owl set up here the birds would leave the grapes alone. What do you think, Silvestro?" Giuseppe called out to his son at the other end of the yard.

"Sure, Papa. That might work." Silvestro answered.

'*Click*' went the sound of the back-gate opening. Giuseppe turned around and there was Stefano, tall and still wearing that big black jacket. Silvestro stepped behind the tree at the end of the yard. He felt safer watching without being seen.

"Giuseppe, have you got something for me? Something green?" Stefano rubbed his hands together in the same way Pasquale had. Silvestro thought, *I have to ask Papa what that finger movement means.*

Giuseppe looked him in the eye and said, "Yes, I do."

He reached into the side of his pants and pulled out his pocket knife. Bending over, Giuseppe quickly cut a bunch of lettuce leaves from their roots. "Here this is good and green." He handed the lettuce to Stefano. "Make sure you rinse it well before eating it."

Silvestro wondered why Stefano just didn't buy the lettuce in the store. He had a nice jacket and fancy shoes. He should have enough money to buy lettuce.

Stefano stepped closer to Silvestro's papa. "Pasquale is not going to like this." Stefano stuck his chest out. "You might want to change your mind."

"That's good lettuce. Tell him it's what I eat." Giuseppe opened the back gate, showing Stefano that he wanted him to leave.

Stefano bumped against Giuseppe on purpose as he walked out. He saw something gray and flat on the ground, bent over and picked it up. "Here. That's what we think of your lettuce." Stefano dropped the lettuce and threw the gray thing at Giuseppe and walked quickly down the alley.

Silvestro came out from hiding behind the tree. He ran up to his Papa who was looking at the gray thing that had bounced off him and was now laying on the ground by his feet. "Papa! It's a dead bird."

Giuseppe bent down to pick it up. "It must have been flattened by one of those cars coming down our alley." Suddenly, Giuseppe burst out laughing. "I know how to fix my bird and grape problem."

The next day Giuseppe told Franco about his meeting with Stefano. "So, you didn't give him any money and he threw a dead bird at you?" Franco asked. "Didn't that scare you?"

"No. I felt good that I didn't give in to those bullies. And the bird was a gift," answered Giuseppe.

"A gift? Are you nuts?"

Giuseppe laughed. "You've got to see what I did. The dead bird is hanging from a string I tied to the middle of my grape arbor. That'll stop the birds from eating my grapes!" Giuseppe was so proud of himself. "I used to do this in Sicily. It helped keep the birds off the grapes."

"I've got to see this." Franco said as he ran through the store to the backyard and into the garden. There in the middle of the grape arbor was the flattened dead bird hanging from a white cotton string. Tied to the string was a small cardboard sign with words written in Italian on it. Franco bent forward and read aloud. "*Se no stai attento, succedera anche a te.* (If you don't watch out, this will happen to you too)."

"Is it working?" Franco asked. Just then a bird landed on the grape arbor and bit a piece out of a ripe green grape.

"Shoo, shoo." Giuseppe waved his hands at the bird. "These dumb American birds. They keep eating my grapes."

Franco burst out laughing, "Giuseppe!" He pointed to the cardboard sign.

"American birds can't read Italian." Franco turned around and laughed all the way back into the store.

Silvestro was quietly eating his breakfast when he heard his papa cry out, "Oh no!"

He slid off his chair and ran down the stairs to find his papa in the store with his hands on his head. The store was a mess. The apple stand was broken and apples were all over the floor. Tomatoes had been crushed against the green tiles on the floor, as if someone had stomped on them to make tomato sauce.

"Silvestro, go get your mama." Giuseppe shakily said.

"Mama, come quick. The store. The store is broken!" Silvestro shouted as he ran back up the stairs.

Rosaria quickly came into the store carrying Gina in her arms. She stopped moving as soon as she saw the mess. Everywhere Rosaria looked fruit and vegetables had been turned over onto the floor and some were smashed. "Our store! Our beautiful store! How did this happen? Who did this?"

"It wasn't me." Silvestro said as he came out from behind his mama.

Just then, the front door swung open and in walked Pasquale, the man with the gray hat.

"Oh Giuseppe," he said. "What a shame. Your nice and tidy market is now a wreck. Looks like you need some protection."

Giuseppe stepped over the fallen pears by his feet. He put his hand on the doorknob of the front door and looking right at Pasquale hissed, "Our store is closed right now, sir. We have some cleaning to do."

"Yes, you do. Think about what I said." Pasquale walked out the door with a smile on his face.

Silvestro bent over and picked up the apple by his feet. "This one's okay, Papa. I'll wipe it and put it back on the stand."

Giuseppe picked up and hugged his son. "You're a good boy, Silvestro. Get your books. I'll walk you to school. Rosaria, leave everything alone until I get back. I'm going to talk to the police."

When Silvestro got home from school, the market was clean and neat again. Franco stopped sweeping the floor to swing Silvestro around him, "How was school today?" he asked.

"Fine," Silvestro answered. "The store is all fixed again. Who messed it up?"

"The police said they don't know. It could have been some kids just being naughty. Don't worry about it. Have a plum." Franco smiled at Silvestro as he gave him the fruit. Time went by and things seemed to be back to normal in the Amatiza Fruit and Vegetable Market. People shopped at the market, Silvestro loved going to school, and Gina liked playing on the shop's floor while her parents worked. One day

Rosaria had news for Giuseppe. "We are going to have another baby, Giuseppe." Rosaria happily looked up at her husband.

"That's wonderful! Another baby." Giuseppe hugged his wife. "Let's tell the kids when Silvestro comes home from school." Giuseppe wanted to see Silvestro's face when he told him he might have another sister or maybe a brother. Silvestro always wanted a brother, even though he liked playing with Gina.

"How about I pack a picnic dinner and we tell them at the park?" Rosaria was excited to tell her children too. "I'll make mortadella sandwiches. Silvestro and Gina love mortadella."

"I do too. Good idea!" Giuseppe gave his wife another hug. The door of the store swung open and in walked Pasquale and Stefano.

"Hello, hello my friends." Pasquale opened his arms as if he was going to hug Rosaria and Giuseppe.

Giuseppe stepped in front of Rosaria, as if protecting her. "What do you want, Pasquale?"

"Giuseppe, Giuseppe, you know what I want. Money. Where is it? You have some for me this time?" Pasquale held his hand out with an open palm.

Giuseppe took two steps toward the front door. He opened it and pointed down the street. "The bank is that way. That's where you go to get money."

"Ah, Giuseppe. You might want to think a little more about this." Pasquale bumped into Giuseppe on purpose as he, Steffano, went out the door.

"Giuseppe, what are we going to do?" Rosaria seemed upset.

"Don't worry." Giuseppe said as he put his arm around his wife. "We are not going to give in to bullies. A bully just keeps going until someone stands up to him. Now, go get the picnic ready. I'm getting hungry. Gina will be waking up from her nap soon and Silvestro will be home from school."

Later that evening, Giuseppe, Rosaria, Silvestro and Gina were walking home from their picnic. Silvestro was singing, "A brother, a brother, I'm finally going to have a brother."

Gina was dancing in front of him yelling, "A sister, a sister. I'm going to have a sister!"

Giuseppe laughed. "You two! It's one baby and we don't know if it's a girl or a boy until it's born."

"Look, Giuseppe." Rosaria called out. "There's a crowd in front of our store. And there's smoke."

Giuseppe ran ahead. "Oh, no! My market!" There, where the green and red striped awning once hung, were black strips of cloth. Looking through the broken windows Giuseppe saw black charred stands which once held fresh shining fruit. "It's gone. It's gone." Giuseppe cried out. "What happened?"

A man who had been part of the watching crowd walked over and put his hand on Giuseppe's shoulder. "The fire department just left. There was a fire."

Silvestro ran up and hugged his Papa's legs. "A fire? Are my toys okay?" Franco bent down and put his arm on Silvestro's shoulder. "They should be. Luckily, it's only downstairs where the shop is. Your home upstairs is still okay." He stood up and spoke to Giuseppe. "The firemen put the fire out before it went upstairs. We didn't know where you were. Come stay with me tonight. Tomorrow you can start cleaning up."

Giuseppe hugged his friend. "Thank you, Franco. You're a good friend."

"That's what friends are for. We help each other when times are tough," Franco said.

It was a few months later when the Amatiza family were standing together against a ship's railing. Gina began to cry when she heard the loud horn from the big ship. "It's okay," said Silvestro as he stroked her arm. "Ships are noisy."

Rosaria rocked Gina on her lap. "I think we made the right decision, Giuseppe. We have family in Sicily. They can help us with our children and the new baby that's coming. My sister writes that things are better there now." Rosaria smiled as she looked out onto the Atlantic Ocean in front of her.

Giuseppe sighed. "I know. I'll miss our store, but there was no way I was going to give that bully Pasquale money. The good thing is we got enough from selling the building to buy a nice almond farm in Ventimiglia."

Silvestro looked up at his papa, "You do like to grow things, Papa." Then he looked back at the buildings of New York City that seemed to be getting smaller and smaller as the ship they were on got further and further away. "But I like America. It is my home. I will come back," he said to himself.

Chicago, 2018

Annie jumped off her Grandmother, Lina's lap. "Those bad guy bullies burned their store? Is that what happened? That's terrible!"

Lina looked at her eight-year-old granddaughter. "No one ever knew for sure. They never found any proof. But my grandparents, Giuseppe and Rosaria believed that Pasquale and Stefano caused that fire."

"So, they left New York and went back to Sicily. I feel sorry for them," Annie said.

"Don't be sad. You and I wouldn't be alive today if they hadn't returned to Sicily." Lina explained. "Remember the new baby they were going to have? That was my papa, Paulo. He was born in Ventimiglia. He grew up and married my mother, Grazia. I wouldn't have been born and your mama and you wouldn't have been born if Giuseppe and his family hadn't gone back to Sicily."

Annie thought for a minute. "They never came back to America, then?"

"Silvestro and Gina did, when they were older. They were born in the United States and were able to come back because of that. So, years later my Uncle Silvestro filled out the papers so his brother, my papa, Paolo and his family could come to America. And here we are!" Lina gave Annie a big hug.

Annie leaned her head against her Grandmother's shoulder, "Thank you for telling me this story. It's wonderful when something good happens after something bad. I am glad Giuseppe went back to Sicily. Because of that, I have you to love me!"

The Suitcase

Chicago, 1964

"When I was in first grade, I drew a picture of a nurse stirring a pot on a kitchen stove. The teacher asked me if I wanted to be a cook, since we were supposed to draw a picture of what we wanted to be when we grew up. I quickly shook my head. No! I wanted to be a nurse and a Mommy who cooked for her family." Lina was telling the story to her best friend, Diane, as they sat next to each other on the bus coming home from school.

"What about now?" Diane asked. "When we were in sixth grade, I remember you talking about wanting to be an archaeologist."

"I am not sure. I know I want to work with kids. I love being with them."

"Well, you sure get to babysit a lot with your younger cousins. Are you thinking about being a teacher? After all, you do like telling people what to do." Diane's eyes twinkled merrily as she teased her friend.

"Nah. Teachers have too many rules to follow. And since I am so bossy, get up. It's our stop." Lina grabbed her backpack and hurried to the door of the bus. Diane quickly followed.

Diane and Lina had become best friends shortly after Lina had moved across the street from her when they were both in sixth grade. Now, they were in their junior year of high school and thinking about college.

"I really have no idea what I want to do after high school," Diane said as she hopped off the high bottom step of the bus. "I think I might just go to a community college while I figure it out. Anyway, we have a whole year yet."

Lina's long brown hair swayed as she shook her head at her friend. "It's better to have a plan, Diane. We can't waste time and money. Not all colleges have degrees in all careers. And my parents won't understand me going to college without it being for something specific."

"Well, maybe we need to do some hunting at the library." Diane's eyebrows raised upward hopefully.

"Ah, you just want to go see that new guy who's working the front desk." Lina teased. "He's kind of cute." Lina was an avid reader and used the local library frequently. Diane had gone with her last week and talked about the young man at the front desk for the whole three blocks on the walk home. "Actually, doing some research at the library is not a bad idea. Thanks, Diane!" Lina hugged her friend before crossing the street to go into her house. "See you tomorrow!" She called over her shoulder as she climbed up the stairs to her brown brick two story house.

"Mama, I'm home," Lina sang out as she walked in the door. No one answered. That was strange. Mama was always home when Lina got home from school. They usually had coffee and cookies together as an afterschool snack. Lina walked into the kitchen and immediately gagged. There was her mother sitting at the kitchen table with her mouth full as she held a banana in her hand. "Yuck!" Lina exclaimed. "I hate bananas! The smell makes me sick."

"I know. I know." Grazia, Lina's mother mumbled as she chewed. She slowly cleared her throat. "The doctor said I should eat half a banana every day. It's supposed to help with the medicines I am taking for my heart."

"Okay, Mama. But can you please eat them while I'm at school? The smell of bananas just makes me want to throw up like I did on the ship when we came from Italy."

"I thought you'd get over that, but it's been ten years and you still have trouble with them. How about I pour you some coffee? That will change the smell. Get the cookies out of the pot."

Lina opened the bottom cabinet next to the sink and pulled out a dented aluminum pasta pot. It was filled to the brim with the plain biscotti cookies they had made yesterday. Lina and her mama made cookies every week and filled the pot. Lina's papa loved these plain cookies and crumbled them into his oversized coffee cup, eating the coffee, cookie, sugar and milk mixture with a spoon every morning and evening. She took a small plate and put two cookies on it. They didn't eat as many of the cookies as her papa did.

"So, how was school?" Grazia asked as she set the blue coffee cup down in front of her daughter.

"Okay. My counselor called me into her office today. She asked me if I was thinking about going to college. She said that my grades are good enough and that I might be able to get a scholarship. Mama, I told her yes. I want to go to college. That's okay isn't it?" Lina's nervous words were coming out faster and faster. She knew her parents had immigrated so she could have a good education, but none of her parents' friends had daughters who had gone to college. The older Italian girls Lina knew worked as secretaries, did office work, or sales clerks in department stores. Lina's parents had been firm on Lina getting good grades and getting a good education so that she didn't have to do factory work like they did.

Grazia took a sip of her coffee and set her cup down. She looked into Lina's hopeful eyes with her own big brown eyes. "We came to America so you could have a better life. And we do have a better life. Now we own our own house, and it is much nicer than the one we had in Ventimiglia. But we've worked very hard, and I can't work anymore. You know that, Lina. My heart. It's weak."

"I know, Mama." Lina put her hand over her mother's.

"It's not fair. I planned to keep working." Grazia frequently spoke with regret about not being able to earn a paycheck anymore. She had her first heart attack a couple of years ago. She had to be very careful and not exert herself too much. "It's just your papa working now. College is expensive. I don't know if we can afford it, Lina."

"That's what the counselor was talking about, Mama. She said I have a good chance of getting the Illinois State Scholarship with my test scores. Also, there are other scholarships I can apply for. And I have money saved up. Of course, I would keep working part time, like I am now." Lina's part time job in the credit department of the Montgomery Ward's department store had made it clear to her that she wanted a career working with people, not just shuffling papers in an office.

"You think that's possible?" Grazia sounded hopeful.

"My counselor thinks so," Lina said.

"Well, let me talk to your papa." Grazia let out a sigh as she cupped Lina's chin with her hand. "If I were you, and had the education you've gotten, I'd want to be a nurse. Just think my daughter could be a nurse." Grazia had a high respect for nurses after spending so much time in the hospital after her first heart attack and repeated hospitalizations.

"I don't know, Mama. I don't think I'd like to change bedpans and wipe butts. But I do think I want to help people. Thanks for talking to Papa." Lina smiled. She knew that if her mama set her mind to it, she could talk her papa into anything.

It was a few days before Lina was able to walk to the library. She figured they would have reference books on occupations and careers. Lina always enjoyed scanning the listings in the card catalog. Frequently, she found something interesting before or after spotting the exact topic she was looking up. There was something comforting in that chest full of little drawers full of cards. It felt like the path to all the information you'd want was in that wooden cabinet. Sometimes, she thought she could be a librarian. She loved being surrounded by books. But in her heart, she knew she couldn't be quiet enough. Lina was loud and loved to talk and sometimes she talked to herself. That wouldn't be good for a librarian.

The reference section in the library was in the front of the building, so Lina decided to look through the shelves with the encyclopedias. Sure enough, there was a big, fat, gray book with the word careers on the spine. Lina pulled the book off the shelf and set it on the rectangular table behind her. She sat in the chair and opened the book. The book felt old and solid, like it was full of wisdom. Just like an encyclopedia, the book was arranged in alphabetical order. Lina turned to 'N' and looked for 'nurse', even though she had told her mother it wasn't what she wanted to do. Maybe there was a kind of nursing that would be right for her. It was worth checking out. At the very end of the section on pediatric nursing there were dark letters that said, See also: Recreational therapist, social worker, speech therapist, etc.

Lina's eyes widened as she saw the word recreational.

"That's playing," she whispered. "You can have a job that pays you to play?" Her fingers quickly ruffled the pages to the 'R' section. She read through the section on recreational therapy. Lina felt herself smiling as she read about the use of play and fun activities to help sick, disabled or injured people get better. *This sounds fun,* Lina thought. She saw the darkened 'See also' section. It listed: Nurse, occupational therapist, social work, speech therapist, etc. Lina had never heard of occupational therapy either. Before she knew it, her fingers were flipping back the pages to the 'O' section. As she read the description, it sounded a little like recreational therapy but more useful. It also was a career where you helped people get better by using activities to make them stronger, but it also helped teach people with injuries or disabilities how to do everyday things, like eating and getting dressed. Lina felt a warmth spreading in her heart as she looked at the photo of an occupational therapist helping a child pull a shirt sleeve over their new arm made of metal. "This is it," Lina said out loud.

"Shush," said the librarian from her nearby desk.

Lina pulled out a pencil and piece of paper from her brown canvas purse. As she copied down the address for the American Occupational Therapy Association, she felt her heart pounding in her chest. "I know what I want to do. Now

I just need to find out how I can become an occupational therapist." She would send out a letter to the association just as soon as she got home. Lina closed the book and carefully placed it back on the shelf. She traced the spine of the book with her finger thinking, *Thank you.*

The next week Grazia placed the mail next to Lina's coffee cup as she waited for her to come home from school. The top letter was addressed to Lina. It was thick and probably full of advertisements, but Grazia was always reluctant to throw out mail until Lina checked it. Her spoken English was getting better, but she was always nervous about reading English.

Lina came in the back-kitchen door and tossed her green backpack in the corner on the floor.

"Hi Mama. You have coffee ready for me. Thanks!" Lina loved their family's ritual of coffee and cookies when they came home from work or school. It used to be milk and cookies when Lina was younger, but her coffee breaks at Montgomery Wards had taught her to enjoy coffee. She slid into her place at the table. Lina picked up the top envelope. It was addressed to her and was from the American Occupational Therapy Association. A big smile spread across her face.

"What is it, Lina?" Grace could see the excitement in her daughter's eyes.

"It's from the therapy association. Remember I told you I was writing to find out about the colleges that teach occupational therapy." Lina explained. There was a brochure about occupational therapy, a list of universities across America where you could major in occupational therapy, as well as the cover letter. Lina handed the brochure to her

Mother. "See, Mama, here are some pictures of what an occupational therapist does." Her mama had a hard time understanding this career. They had never heard of therapists in her mountain village in Sicily. The town didn't even have a doctor.

Unfortunately, her mama was familiar with hospitals in America, but her experiences had all been with nurses and doctors. It was hard for her to understand this career that Lina was excited about. Grazia looked through the brochure. She saw a woman holding a child who was seated on a big ball. Another woman was helping a man put on his shirt, and another woman was fastening what looked like a white brace onto a woman's hand. It just looked like they were helpers, kind of like the nurse's aides in the hospital. "Wouldn't it be better just to be a nurse, Lina? It seems like that would be more important than just helping. You don't need to go to college to help people get dressed," she said as she handed Lina back the brochure.

"Mama, it's not just helping. It's teaching so people can do it themselves. It's about helping people be as independent as possible." Lina explained. She was looking at the list of universities. They were organized by state. There was one listing under Illinois, the University of Illinois in Champaign-Urbana. "Oh, no," slipped out of Lina's mouth. Her parents didn't approve of girls living away from their home. Good Italian girls lived at home until they got married. They didn't get their own apartments or go away to college. Actually, none of her parents' friends had daughters that went to college. Some had gone to hairdresser's school or taken a secretarial course after high school, but that was about it.

"I'm going for a walk, Mama." Lina scooped up her mail and quickly went out the back door. She needed to think and she wasn't ready to explain things to her mother.

Lina walked to the nearby city park. There was a green wooden bench under a big elm tree that faced the playground. Sometimes Lina came here when she had to think things through. The tree was like an old friend. Looking up at the blue sky through the green leaves and branches overhead had a calming effect on Lina. And sometimes the voices of children playing on the slide and swings helped Lina remember how lucky she was. Had her family stayed in Ventimiglia, she wouldn't have had playgrounds to play on as a child or one to take her own children to. She plopped down on the bench. *Why?* She thought. *There were so many colleges in Chicago. Why didn't one of them teach occupational therapy?*

This is a new career. It's only been around since the 1920s. That was only forty some years ago.

Her brain doing what it always did, answering questions and looking at the other side.

Lina took a deep breath. She couldn't change the college situation. "What can I change?" Lina asked out loud.

You can pick a different career or you can change what you think about going away to college.

Lina's brain answered her.

Lina still had the brochure in her hand. She looked at the pictures of therapists helping people become more independent. "I want this. I want to be an occupational therapist." Lina seemed even more sure. "I can be independent too. I can do this. I'm not afraid to go to college in Champaign-Urbana."

Lina looked up through the leaves of the tree.

Honey, your fear is not the problem. It's your parents' fear. They are afraid you won't be thought of as a respectable Italian girl. It's not what they've grown up with.

Sighing. "I am respectable. I will be respectable, even if I go away to college."

If you go away? How about when? You just said, you can do this.

Sometimes Lina hated it when her brain threw something, she said back at her.

I can do this, Lina thought. *I can go away to college and pay my own way. I'll get a scholarship and use the money I have saved. And I'll keep working part time while I am in school. I'll just tell my mama and papa that this is what I have to do.* Lina felt sure about her choice. She got up from the bench and brushed her hand against the trunk of the tree. "Thanks," she whispered to the tree.

Diane slid into the seat next to Lina on the bus. "So, how did it go? Did you tell your parents about going to college in Champaign?"

Lina groaned. "It was awful. They just don't understand. Thankfully, they're still onboard about me going to college. I was afraid they would start to object to that too." Lina turned

65

in her seat so that she was looking right into Diane's blue eyes. "Do you know that my Uncle Silvestro yelled at my dad? He said it was a waste to send a girl to college! He thinks my dad is being uppity for wanting me to go to college. Can you believe that?"

Diane gently shook her head, "Some people. Thank goodness he's not your dad."

"Mama and Papa are both hounding me about picking a different career and to go to school somewhere in Chicago so I can live at home. Papa just said: 'No. You're not going away'." Lina's voice was getting louder as she remembered the argument from the night before.

"What did you say?" Diane asked.

Lina took a deep breath, "I said, I'm sorry, Papa but I am going. I can pay my own way and I'll be eighteen. Occupational therapy is what I want to study."

"Gee! What did your papa do?" Diane was aware of how old-fashioned Lina's parents could be. She knew that a 'good Italian girl' didn't disagree with her parents.

"He slammed the door and went out for a walk. Papa was really mad. He didn't talk to me the rest of the night or this morning. It makes me sad, but it's what I expected."

Diane patted Lina's hand. "What about your mom? Was she as upset as your dad?"

"It was different with Mama. She seemed really sad. That actually hurt more," Lina rubbed the corner of her eye.

"Are you crying?" Diane asked. "I have Kleenex in my purse."

"No. I am not going to cry over this." Lina sighed. "It's my future and my life. I have to be strong. I have to look forward." Lina took a deep breath. "Mama was talking about nursing school again this morning. I tried to explain how important this is to me. That I am not wanting to go away to college because I think it'll be fun."

"But it will be," interrupted Diane.

"That's not it. It's because I don't have a choice. It's the only school in Illinois that you can go to in order to become an OT."

"What's an OT? Now, I'm confused."

"That's short for occupational therapist. I have been doing more reading on it. The guidance counselor at school got me more information. The more I find out, the more I think it's right for me. I tried to explain more of it to Mama this morning. She just kept shaking her head and saying, 'Wouldn't nursing be good enough?'"

Diane chuckled, "So, instead of changing bed pans, you'll be teaching people how to pull their pants down so they can use a toilet. Still sounds gross to me."

Lina laughed, "Thanks, Diane. I needed that. Let's change the subject. Are you coming to my birthday party next week? It's just my parents, my Aunt Marianna and Uncle Nicasio, and my cousins. My dad's still mad at my Uncle Silvestro, so he's not invited."

"Those are your aunt and uncle and cousins who recently came from Italy, right?"

"Yea. You haven't seen them in a while. My cousin's English is really coming along. It's pretty funny that my cousin Cecelia can sing all these American songs that are on the radio but she doesn't really know what all the words mean. She has a nice voice, though."

"Yeah, I'll come. And let's get moving. There's the school. We have to get off the bus."

Paolo carried the bag of cotton balls into the kitchen and set them down onto the brown Formica table top. "Here, they are. Use these to stuff one cannoli."

"What?" Grazia exclaimed as she set down the delicate cannoli shell, she was about to stuff with cannoli filling.

"I want to play a joke on Nicasio. He used to always play pranks on me in Ventimiglia. Here's my chance to get back at him. Take a cannoli shell and put some cotton balls in the middle, then put the filling over the ends so he can't see the cotton balls. He'll bite into it and get cotton!" Paolo slapped his thigh and laughed. "It will be so funny. I am going to love seeing his face."

Lina looked at her mama in surprise. Her papa didn't play practical jokes on people. She picked up another cannoli shell and slowly started spooning the filling into it.

"Okay, Paolo. I'll do it. I'll set it on a separate plate in the refrigerator next to the regular cannoli so somebody else doesn't eat it by mistake. But if he chokes, you have to get the cotton out of his mouth." Grazia took two cotton balls out of the bag and carefully poked them into the center of the cannoli shell. Paolo watched carefully, as if he wasn't sure his wife knew how to stuff a cannoli. She quickly covered the ends with the usual cannoli filling and sprinkled some powdered sugar over the top. Lina held out a small white plate to her mama. Grazia put the cannoli on the plate and handed it to Paolo. "There. Put it in the refrigerator and leave me alone so Lina and I can finish the rest. And take those cotton balls with you." When Paolo left the room, Grazia looked at Lina and said, "Your Uncle Nicasio and your papa used to play jokes on each other at their farms. Once your Uncle Nicasio wrote a love poem and tied it to your papa's donkey. It was supposed to be from your Uncle Nicasio's donkey. Stuff like that."

Lina thought, *That's the happiest I have seen Papa since I told him about going to Champaign. He's been so mad at me. I am not going to talk about college today. It's my birthday and I want my family to be happy.*

Later that evening, Lina was seated on the sofa with her friend Diane and her cousins, when Paolo walked into the living room with a tray piled high with cannoli.

"Who wants cannoli?" Paolo asked. "Here, take this big one, Nicasio." Paolo handed his brother-in-law the specially prepared cannoli. "Grazia's cannoli are really good. What do you think?" Paolo stood back to watch as Nicasio took a bite. Lina stopped talking to watch her uncle chew. She waited for him to say something about the cotton ball. Nicasio chewed, swallowed, and took another bite.

Lina was puzzled. *Did her papa give her Uncle Nicasio a real cannolo instead of the one stuffed with cotton balls?* She thought. Lina watched her papa lean forward and stare at her uncle's mouth as he ate the cannoli.

Nicasio popped the last bit of cannoli in his mouth and licked his fingertip, "Mm, that was the best cannoli I've ever had!" and he slapped Paolo on his back.

Paolo couldn't stand it anymore, "How did you eat that? There was cotton in there!"

"I wasn't going to let you win. I knew you were going to prank me sometime soon. I could see it in your face when you brought in the cannoli. So, I just ate it." Nicasio burst out laughing. "You should have seen your face, Paolo. You'd think your mouth was full of the cotton balls! Jokes on you, after all!" Paolo and Nicasio's laughter filled the house.

"It was wonderful to see her papa laughing," Lina smiled as she munched on her cannoli. "Hurry up, Lina. It's time to open your birthday presents." Came Grazia's voice from the kitchen. They all crowded into the kitchen where several wrapped packages were on the kitchen table. Lina sat at the table and picked up a square box wrapped in pink flowered paper.

"That's from me," said Diane.

Lina quickly tore off the paper. She loved the sound the ripping made. Inside the box was a denim shoulder strap purse. "Oh, thanks, Diane. I love it!"

"I thought you could use another purse. It's fun to change them once in a while." Diane loved purses and had them in several colors. "Open that big one next. I want to see what's in it." Diane pointed to the very large box wrapped in red striped paper.

Pulling the box toward her, Lina said, "It's not so heavy for such a large box." She couldn't imagine what was in it. "Who's it from?" Lina asked as she looked around the room.

"Me," Grazia said as she smiled at her daughter.

Lina tossed the crumpled ripped paper into the garbage can under the sink behind her. She put her hands on the lid of the box and lifted it up. "Ohhhh. It's a suitcase. A green suitcase!"

"I thought you would need one when you go to college in Champagne," Grazia softly said leaning in toward her daughter and she kissed her on the head. "Happy Birthday, Lina."

For once in her life, Lina was speechless. She threw her arms around her mama's neck as tears started to fill the corners of her eyes.

"I think she likes it," Uncle Nicasio said.

"Oh, Mama. Papa. It's all right then? You're happy?" Lina gushed with joy as she ran her hand over the top of the suitcase.

"No. We're not happy." Lina's papa growled under his breath. "But it is alright." Grazia smiled. "We've talked about it. You can study to be a therapist."

"An occupational therapist," Lina smiled. "Thank you, Mama for the suitcase and thank you, Papa, for bringing us to America!"

Red Rubber Ball

Chicago, 1972

"Call the priest. I don't have much time." My mama's voice cracked as she lay back upon the hospital's fluffed pillows. "Call him, now, Lina!" Even with a weak heart, my mama could still command a room. "I need to confess before surgery."

"Mama, I'll call him, but I can't promise he can make it in time. Your heart surgery is scheduled for early tomorrow morning." The sterile walls and furnishings didn't help my sinking spirits. I didn't want to disappoint my mother. "Call him. It's important. I can't talk to the hospital priest. My English isn't good enough." Pleaded my mama in her heavily Italian accented English. "I can't have the surgery without my confession!"

As I stepped out of the hospital room into the brightly lit hallway, to phone our parish church's Italian speaking, priest, Father Giovanni, I wondered what Mama would be so worried about confessing. In the 25 years I've had with her, she's never done anything that should worry her so much. Grazia Amatiza led a good life. *There was no one kinder and more giving than my mama,* I thought. A heart valve replacement is a serious surgery but doctors do this, every day. I tried to reassure myself as I walked out of the hospital room looking for a phone. There was one in the waiting room at the end of the hall. Catholicism is important in Italian culture, I told myself as I searched in my wallet for a quarter. I dialed the numbers for St Cecilia's Church. Listening to the phone ringing at the other end, I thought, *Mama couldn't have done anything that bad.*

Thankfully, an hour later, Father Giovanni knocked on the door of Mama's room. He was tall for an Italian with a lanky build, but had the thick dark brown hair and the brown eyes people expect of most Italians.

Father Giovanni didn't wait for either of us to respond, but strode quickly across the room to the bed, "*Grazia, como ti senti*? (Grace, how do you feel)," he asked as he bent over and laid his hand gently on the top of my mama's thinning curly gray hair.

Mama smiled, and as always, the room lit up. "Ah, not too good, but I am still alive," answered Mama in Italian with one of our family's familiar sayings. "Father, I need to confess, please."

"Lina, can you leave us for a bit? Please close the door," said Father Giovanni as he gently sat down in the chair I had just vacated. I picked up my paperback book and my purse and slouched out of the room, pulling the door behind me. Plop! My book fell out of my hand and wedged down between the jamb and the door, leaving it slightly open. I bent down to pick up the book, and felt the hard-plastic edge of the seat of the chair I had set outside the door the night before when making room for me to spend the night. The next thing I knew; I was sitting on that institutional plastic chair with my red clutch purse on my lap while I leaned in toward the slight opening of the doorway of Mama's hospital room.

"Lina," I said to myself, "if you're quiet, you can hear what Mama's so worried about." Being quiet wasn't something that came to me easily, but this felt important. I knew walking away was the ethical thing to do, but I couldn't. I wanted to know what weighed so heavily on Mama's conscience. She seemed so worried.

"Bless me Father, for I have sinned," croaked my Mama's familiar but weakened voice through the crack in the door. I adjusted my posture and placed my open purse on my lap with my fingers inside it, as if looking for something, so anyone walking past would not realize I was eavesdropping. Just another family member waiting outside a loved one's room.

"My last confession was too long ago to remember." Mama paused.

"That's not important, Grazia. We are here with God now." Father Giovanni's calm voice came through the door. For a relatively young priest, he sounded very reassuring and capable.

Mama continued, "I want to tell you about something I did a long time ago back in Ventimiglia, Sicily. It was when my daughter, Lina, was only a little girl." Mama's voice cracked as she spoke. I began to think back too. I was seven years old when we immigrated to the United States. There wasn't much I remembered about our life in that mountain village in Sicily.

"Go on." Father Giovanni's voice interrupted my memories. He laid his hand firmly on top of Grazia's work-worn fingers and listened to her story.

Sicily, 1954

74

"Can I go out? Can I? Can I?" Lina pleaded as she held her mother's face in her delicate little hands.

"In a minute, Lina. I need to braid your hair first." Grazia picked up the brush and ran it gently through Lina's long, thick hair.

"Ouch!" Lina yelped at a knot in her hair, as she bent over to pick up her new red rubber ball.

"Sit still and it won't hurt. Leave the ball alone. You can play with it outside, when I'm done." Grazia was mentally cataloging the long list of tasks she had to do today to get ready for their upcoming move to the United States. Having Lina out of the house would be helpful. Grazia quickly braided Lina's hair into two plaits down her back. "Go outside."

As she patted Lina's little behind toward the beaded doorway. "And be careful," she nudged. "Don't bounce your ball by the bridge. You don't want it to go over and lose it. Papa can't bring you another one from Palermo."

"I know, Mama," Lina retorted. "Papa's never brought me a toy from Palermo before! I'll be careful." Lina ran out into the warm Sicilian sunshine. She was so excited to have a ball to play with. It fit perfectly in her hand and felt so delightfully squishy when she squeezed it.

Lina turned her head toward the 'clackety swoosh' of Conchetta's red and blue beaded curtain in the neighbor's doorway. People left their doors open in their little town of Ventimiglia, but a curtain of plastic beads covered the opening, giving a sense of privacy. Conchetta was carrying out her padded yellow vinyl kitchen chair while her crochet project was tossed over her stooped left shoulder.

"Lina, what do you have there?" she asked as she tilted her chin up to eye the item in Lina's hands.

Slowly, Lina opened her fingers revealing the red rubber ball. "My Papa brought me this from Palermo. He went there yesterday to get the papers for America!"

Conchetta sighed as she settled her arthritic bones into the chair. "Everyone's leaving for America. This street will be empty soon." She took out her crochet hook from the pocket of the universal black dress. Her husband had died five years ago and Conchetta still wore the black dresses of mourning seen throughout the streets of Ventimiglia.

Lina held up her ball so Conchetta could see it. "Do they have red rubber balls like this in America? Look!" Lina bounced the ball down hard in front of Conchetta. "See how high it goes." The ball bounced as high as the small wrought iron balcony of Conchetta's second floor bedroom. Lina caught the ball and looked down the street. The concrete two story houses were like one long building going all the way down the street, each with a separate doorway for the owner's donkey that took the men back and forth to their mountain farms, and the beaded doorway for the family. The narrow, crumbling sidewalks were terraced into steps along the steeply inclined street which seemed to stretch into the dusty yellow mountain beyond.

"Are there mountains in America, Conchetta? Can I bounce my ball into the mountains in America, too?" Lina rattled on endlessly. She was very excited about her upcoming trip.

"How do I know?" groaned Conchetta. "I've never been there. Play with your ball and enjoy the sun. I doubt they have fresh air and sun like we do!"

Lina skipped down the center of the cobblestone street, lightly tossing the red rubber ball up into the warm air and catching it. She began tossing it a little higher and higher each time. Children played in the middle of the street. No one had cars. The only hazards were the occasional donkey droppings.

"Augghh," Lina screamed out as she stubbed her toe against a broken cobblestone. Down she went on her hands and bony knees. The ball came down inches in front of her and merrily bounced its way down the street. It rolled its way to a small curb outside of Sarucha's house. Lina pulled herself up, brushing the dirt off her hands onto her green plaid dress.

Lina's classmate, Sarucha, parted her gray and white beaded doorway curtain. She immediately spied the red rubber ball resting against the curb and snatched the ball up like a fisherman netting sardines from the sea. Lina ran to Sarucha, smiling. "Thanks for getting my ball. I dropped it," she said.

Sarucha clutched the ball tight against the blue flowers of her cotton dress "Your ball?" she snorted as she tossed back her mop of curly black hair. "This is my ball. I left it out here last night." Sarucha smoothly slid the ball into the big side pocket of her dress and clamped her hand over it.

Lina stamped her foot. "No, you didn't! That's my ball! I just dropped it. It's mine!" Her voice grew more shrill with each word. Sarucha took a step back toward her doorway. "No, it's not. It's mine!"

'Clackety swoosh', the doorway curtain parted again and Stella, Sarucha's mother walked out wiping her hands on her flour splattered apron. "What's all the yelling about? What happened?"

"Sarucha took my ball," screeched Lina as Sarucha simultaneously yelled, "It's my ball, Mama. Lina wants my ball!"

"*Basta* (Enough)!" Stella wedged herself between the girls, placing her hands on each girl's panting chest. "Where's the ball?"

Sarucha slowly pulled the ball out of her pocket. "It's mine!" she boldly shouted. Stella deftly plucked the ball from Sarucha's fingers. "Lina, what happened?" Stella bent down to look into Lina's angry blue eyes.

"I was playing with my ball that Papa brought me from Parlemo, when I fell down. I couldn't catch it and it rolled to your house. Sarucha picked it up and said it's hers!" Lina's voice became angrier as the words spilled faster and faster out of her mouth. "It's not hers. It's mine!" Lina's foot again stomped the cobblestone with the last word.

"Basta, Lina. Calm down." Stella said quietly. She turned her head. "Now, Sarucha, you, tell me what happened."

Sarucha looked up at her mother. "I left the ball outside last night. I know I should have brought it into the house. I just forgot. I picked it up and Lina started yelling that the ball was hers. It's mine, Mama." Sarucha tilted her head to the side and looked up with all the innocence of a newborn baby.

Stella turned to Lina. "There. It's Sarucha's." She handed the red rubber ball to Sarucha. "Lina, your ball must have rolled somewhere else. Go look over the bridge." All three of their faces turned to look at the foot and a half high small concrete bridge that spanned a wide ditch crossing the town's main street.

"Come, Sarucha. It's time for your lunch." Stella put her hand on Sarucha's back and guided her into their house.

Lina heard the 'clackety swoosh' of the beads as her mouth fell open. For once in her short seven-year-old life, she was speechless.

Tears rained down from Lina's eyes as she slowly trudged home. Her head was leaning forward against her thin chest. By the time she pushed aside her beaded curtain, Lina was shaking with sobs. "Mama!" She ran into the room, throwing her arms around her mama's waist.

"What happened?" Grazia set aside the shirt that she had been folding to place into the metal brown trunk that was going to America with them. Lina climbed into her mama's lap. Between sobs, she told her mama about the theft and the lie Sarucha had spun. Grazia patted the top of Lina's head.

"Don't worry, Lina. I'll take care of this." She slid Lina from her lap and untied her apron. Grazia scooped Lina's small hand into hers. "Let's go." Pulling Lina down the street, Grazia made her way to the offender's house.

"Stella?" Grazia called out as she stepped through the grey and white beaded doorway. Lina trembled in her mama's grip. She could tell her mama was angry; and when Mama was angry, watch out!

Stella was sitting at her wooden kitchen table snapping the ends off of green beans. Grazia stood with the table between her and Stella. "That was Lina's ball. Paolo brought it from Palermo. Sarucha needs to give it back." Grazia demanded.

"It's Sarucha's ball," Stella calmly responded. "She left it out last night. I don't know what happened to Lina's ball. Go look in the street." She waved a green bean toward the open doorway. "It's not Sarucha's fault if Lina loses things."

Sarucha sat on the floor behind her mother, rolling the red rubber ball back and forth between her skinny outstretched legs. She looked up at Lina and stuck her tongue out at her.

Lina stamped her foot and pointed at the ball, "Mama, look."

Grazia looked down at the red ball. "That's Lina's. I have never seen Sarucha playing with a red ball before. That's the one Paolo bought. It's Lina's." She bent down toward the ball to take it from Sarucha.

Stella aggressively plucked the ball up before Grazia could grab it. She placed it into her apron pocket and kept her hand over it. "One red ball looks like another. This is Sarucha's. Don't you have packing to do?"

Defeated, Grazia turned Lina's shoulders toward the doorway. Her voice shook from her seething anger, "I am glad to be leaving! Leaving this street! Leaving lying people like you!" Fiercely swatting the grey and white beads curtain, she guided Lina out the doorway.

Tears rolled down Lina's face. Between gritted teeth, Grazia uttered "Don't worry, Lina. When we get to America, I'll buy you a red ball. A better ball, better than any ball Sarucha and Stella will ever see!" The words seemed intended as much for herself as for Lina.

The next morning Lina sat between Grazia's feet. "Ouch!" Lina yelped as Grazia tugged on her hair to neatly braid it.

"You yell ouch every time I braid your hair and I never hurt you," said Grazia.

"Well, I am hurt. My head hurts and my heart hurts too!" Lina said with the kind of fury only a child possesses.

"Your heart hurts?" Grazia was now worried. She peered down into Lina's face as she gently laid her hand on Lina's chest.

"Yes. Sarucha lied and took my ball. My heart hurts now." Lina's voice ran from anger to pure sadness.

"Ohhh, daughter of mine, believe me. It will be okay. There will be plenty of red balls in America. Now, go play. I have work to do." Grazia bent down to pick up the pitcher. "I have to go get some water at the pump. Stay inside while I am gone." Grazia started walking through the beaded curtain. Looking back at Lina's sad face she said, "And don't touch anything inside the trunk. I am packing it for the ship to America." Grazia strode out into the middle of the street and looked down toward the pump. Stella was walking toward the pump as well. Sarucha was at her side tossing the red rubber ball up in the air and catching it with both hands. Grazia fumed, muttering under her breath. "I bet she stole it. How dare they take my Lina's ball!" Then she thought, *but maybe Sarucha also had a red ball. The stalls in Palermo are filled with them.*

"Grazia, how are you?" called Conchetta from her crocheting spot next to her doorway.

Grazia strode up to Conchetta. She took a deep breath and said "I'm a little upset. Lina lost the ball Paulo brought her from Parlemo. She said Sarucha took it."

Conchetta shook her head gently. "Kids. They're always doing something naughty." Conchetta looked down the street toward Stella and Sarucha's house. "I saw Lina playing with her ball. She missed the catch and it bounced on the cobblestones and stopped in front of Stella's house."

"Did Sarucha pick up Lina's ball?" Grazia asked. The anger started to rise up again.

"I don't know. I went inside to get another skein of yarn. I'm making a shawl." Conchetta proudly held up the partially made black and white striped shawl.

"Pretty. *Ciao* (good bye)," Grazia uttered as she stomped down the street glaring at Stella and Sarucha at the bottom of the hill. Stella was gossiping with the other women by the water pump. Sarucha was showing the ball to another little girl at the pump. Grazia marched down the street with a determined gait. "I'm getting that ball back. How dare they lie to me and Lina. Sarucha is a little girl. God knows the children in this miserable little village don't have enough toys to play with. But Stella! She's a grown up. She should know better. How dare she steal from Lina!" Grazia became angrier and angrier. Walking past Stella's house, she looked at the curb where Lina's ball must have come to rest in front of Stella's house. Looking up she saw that their beaded curtain had caught on the back of a chair just to the inside of the doorway. There on the kitchen table in front of her was Stella's pasta pot. Without thinking, Grazia took two steps into Stella's kitchen, grabbed the pot and turned quickly back up the street. "That'll show her," Grazia thought as she swung the shiny pot through her own beaded doorway. No one was in her kitchen. Good. Lina must be playing in the bedroom.

Grazia lifted the heavy brown lid on the trunk. She picked up the neatly folded clothes and set the tall aluminum pasta pot with copper handles into the bottom of the trunk. Lina's folded dresses fit neatly into the pot. Laying her own dresses over the pot, Grazia thought, *No one will see it. Thank goodness Conchetta had gone back inside her house. She didn't see me with the pot. Stella took my daughter's ball. I took her pot. That's the end of it!* Grazia slammed the lid down on the trunk.

Chicago,1972

"She stole the pasta pot!" Lina gasped as her hand covered her mouth. "My mother!" Lina was astounded. Her mother was always adamant about doing the right thing. "Why, she made me return the candy bar I took from the grocery store when I was just three years old." Lina remembered the red rubber ball and Sarucha's theft. She had chalked it up to childhood shenanigans.

The tall aluminum cookie pot had always been in the bottom cabinet to the right of the sink. It was always filled with cookies we made for Papa and for company. For as long as Lina could remember her mama would make the plain biscotti cookies shaped into a log or an 'S'. Papa would eat them every morning and afternoon by dunking them into his coffee. Sometimes he would crumble them into the coffee cup and make a cookie coffee mash. He ate so many that Lina and Mama used five pounds of flour a week to make the cookies. Of course, they always had them on hand for when people came over to visit. The cookie pot was a staple in Mama's kitchen. But it was Stella's pot!

Grazia's wavering voice broke into Lina's thoughts in her seat outside the hospital room. "I stole the pot and I wasn't sorry. In the beginning, it made me happy to see that pot in my house. I felt justified. The children in our village didn't have many toys. The ball was important to Lina. Stella and Sarucha lying to her was wrong. It made me so mad, but I …" Grazia looked up to Father Giovanni.

"How do you feel now, Grazia? Now is what's important to you and to God," came Father Giovanni's calm voice.

"Now, I am scared. I did wrong. I did a bad thing but the worst is that I was proud of it. Father, I may not live through the surgery tomorrow. Can I be forgiven?" Grazia's voice sounded like that of a child.

"Grazia, let's pray together for forgiveness."

Lina could hear the soft murmur of Father Giovanni's prayer and her mother's shaking voice; she turned her head away. It felt wrong to hear their prayers. Suddenly, Father Giovanni's voice came clearly through the cracked open door,

"So, now what are you going to do to make this better?" he asked.

"Better?" Grazia was puzzled. "I've asked for forgiveness. I am sorry. The pot is in my kitchen. It was a long time ago. The pot has dents now. I don't know if Stella is still in Ventimiglia. And I am having heart surgery tomorrow."

"I know all this, Grazia," Father Giovanni continued. "But sometimes true forgiveness requires us to do something to make it right. Think about it. When you are healed, after the surgery, do something. Some ideas will come to you that will help you to know that you can make it right."

"I will try, Father. I will try," Grazia whispered.

Lina heard Father Giovanni bless her mother with the sign of the cross. She thought, *I better move from here. I don't want them to know I was listening.* Bending down, she gently picked up the book stuck between the door and the doorjamb. Quietly, Lina stepped away from the door and began to walk down the hall. *Do something to make it right,* Lina thought. *Hmmm. I didn't expect a task on a pre-surgery confession. But then, maybe it would give her mom something else to hold onto. Something else Grazia had to do might give her mother some strength to endure what was coming,* Lina hoped.

Ventimiglia, Sicily 1973

The colored lights were strung diagonally across the piazza in front of the Church of the Sacred Heart. It looked like a rainbow of X's across the sky. The villagers were beginning to set up their wares for Ventimiglia's patron saint day, Santa Rosalia. There were booths with the usual trinkets like magnets with a Sicilian cart on it or multicolored beaded bracelets. A group of locals were walking slowly down the middle of the street toward the piazza when a honking car horn disturbed their chatter. A red Fiat parted the pedestrians and slowed to a stop next to the piazza.

The door to the red car opened and a tall man with dark blonde hair got out of the car. The man walked around the car and opened the passenger side door. Out stepped Lina, with a look of wonder on her face. "Oh, Tim, it looks so much smaller than I remembered," said Lina to her husband.

"Of course," Tim said. "You were just a child when you last saw your hometown."

"Let's walk around a little before we open the trunk." Lina took off in the direction of her childhood home, in her t-shirt, jeans and athletic shoes. Tim was equally casually dressed which set them even more apart from the villagers who were dressed in their Sunday best for the festival. "I remember our house was just a little past that bridge."

"Bridge?" questioned Tim as he looked all around him.

"There," said Lina as she pointed to a rounded bump in the street that traversed a narrow ditch.

Within minutes the couple strode past the bridge and stopped in front of a small two-story concrete house with a wooden brown door. "It may have been this one. I am not sure."

The brown door opened and out stepped an elderly woman dressed in black. "Can I help you?" she asked Lina suspiciously.

"I am Lina. Lina Amatiza. I lived in Ventimiglia when I was a little girl. My home was on this street." Lina spoke in her rusty Sicilian dialect which she hadn't used in quite a while.

"Ohhh," the elderly lady quickly relaxed and stepped toward Lina, taking Lina's hand into her wrinkled fingers. "Who was your mama and papa?"

Lina smiled, "Grazia Camararie and Paulo Amatiza. We left for America when I was just seven years old."

"Grazia and Paolo? I remember them! Your mother made the best biscotti. She would always share them. How are they? I'm Enza Scarpella. You tell your mother I said hello." The elderly lady in the black cotton dress gushed.

Tim put his arm around Lina, as she looked down at Signora Scarpella. "They've died. My father died of cancer five years ago. And my mother, last year." Lina took a deep breath. "She had heart disease and needed surgery. She came through the surgery, but died of a stroke two months later."

Signora Scarpella patted Lina's hand. "I'm so sorry. Grazia had a good heart. She was a kind woman."

"Thank you. Signora, do you know which was our house?" Lina asked.

"It was this one, next door." Signora Scarpella pointed to the house next door that had red geraniums on the wrought iron balcony.

Tim took Lina's picture in front of the house and then pointed down toward the piazza. The sound of an accordion player wafted up the street. "Looks like things are starting up."

People had gathered in the piazza and were standing in small groups talking with each other. A tall pole had been erected in one corner of the piazza with bags stuffed with candy or a dead rabbit hanging from the top of the pole. Lina explained to Tim how the young men took turns climbing up the greased pole and trying to break the bags with a stick to release the candy sometimes got skunked with the dead rabbit.

Lina and Tim returned to the red Fiat and Tim opened the packed trunk. He removed three big pasta pots each filled with red rubber balls, placing the pots at Lina's feet. Tim looked into Lina's brown eyes. "Ready?"

"I guess so. I am glad there are so many children here at the festival." Lina picked a red ball out of the pasta pot. "This is for you, Mama! I hope it makes it right." Lina tossed the first of many balls to the children in the piazza.